NUTRITION AND
YOUR BODY

YOUR
BODY ON
CARBOHYDRATES

BY ALEXIS BURLING

CONTENT CONSULTANT
Debbie Fetter, PhD
Lecturer (PSOE), Department of Nutrition
University of California, Davis

Cover image: Potatoes are one of many sources
of carbohydrates.

Core Library

An Imprint of Abdo Publishing
abdobooks.com

abdocorelibrary.com

Published by Abdo Publishing, a division of ABDO, PO Box 398166, Minneapolis, Minnesota 55439. Copyright © 2020 by Abdo Consulting Group, Inc. International copyrights reserved in all countries. No part of this book may be reproduced in any form without written permission from the publisher. Core Library™ is a trademark and logo of Abdo Publishing.

Printed in the United States of America, North Mankato, Minnesota
022019
092019

THIS BOOK CONTAINS RECYCLED MATERIALS

Cover Photo: Nataliia Pyzhova/Shutterstock Images
Interior Photos: Nataliia Pyzhova/Shutterstock Images, 1; iStockphoto, 4–5, 12–13, 15, 17; Burwell Photography/iStockphoto, 7; Lauri Patterson/iStockphoto, 10, 45; Shutterstock Images, 18, 20–21; Warren Goldswain/iStockphoto, 22, 43; Vladislav Noseek/Shutterstock Images, 25; Michael Jung/iStockphoto, 28–29; Red Line Editorial, 31; Jamie Cross/Shutterstock Images, 34; Palino Spisiak/Shutterstock Images, 36–37; Copyright © 2011 Harvard University. For more information about The Healthy Eating Plate, please see The Nutrition Source, Department of Nutrition, Harvard T. H. Chan School of Public Health, http://www.thenutritionsource.org and Harvard Health Publications, health.harvard.edu, 38

Editor: Marie Pearson
Series Designer: Claire Vanden Branden

Library of Congress Control Number: 2018965873

Publisher's Cataloging-in-Publication Data

Names: Burling, Alexis, author.
Title: Your body on carbohydrates / by Alexis Burling.
Description: Minneapolis, Minnesota : Abdo Publishing, 2020 | Series: Nutrition and your body | Includes online resources and index.
Identifiers: ISBN 9781532118838 (lib. bdg.) | ISBN 9781532173011 (ebook) | ISBN 9781644940747 (pbk.)
Subjects: LCSH: Carbohydrates, Refined--Physiological effect--Juvenile literature. | Carbohydrates in the body--Juvenile literature. | Carbohydrates in human nutrition--Juvenile literature. | Food--Health aspects--Juvenile literature.
Classification: DDC 613.20--dc23

CONTENTS

WHAT ARE CARBOHYDRATES?

Many kids love sugary sweets and salty snacks. In the United States, 34 percent of adolescents eat junk food every day. These treats include cookies and potato chips. They have few nutrients but many calories. They have an unhealthy effect on the body. But other foods, such as leafy greens and whole grains, are healthy. They give the body fuel.

Imagine the following scene: A ten-year-old girl named Lucy is participating in a track-and-field meet at school. She is competing in the 60-meter dash. She wants to get the fastest time. That morning, Lucy woke

Foods give the body the energy it needs to work.

up tired. But she ate a bagel with peanut butter and a banana-and-kale smoothie for breakfast. She headed to her race knowing she had eaten just how her coach taught her. In the moments before the starting whistle blows, Lucy's mind is focused. Her body feels energized. When Lucy crosses the finish line, she is in first place.

The changes in Lucy's body happened because of the carbohydrates in her breakfast. Carbohydrates, commonly called carbs, are nutrients found in certain foods. Carbs provide the body with energy. The body's central nervous system, kidneys, brain, and muscles need carbs to function.

HOW CARBS WORK

There are two main types of carbs: simple and complex. Simple carbs are sugars. Complex carbs can be grouped into starches and fibers.

The body breaks down carbs into sugar during digestion. This type of sugar is called glucose. First the glucose travels to the small intestine. Then it is

Bread is a common source of carbs.

absorbed into the bloodstream. When people eat carbs, glucose levels in the blood rise.

As glucose levels rise, the pancreas makes a hormone called insulin. Insulin tells cells in the muscles, liver, tissues, and fat to absorb the glucose. These cells

HIGH AND LOW BLOOD SUGAR

One of the body's most important functions is regulating glucose levels in the blood. If levels soar or drop too much, there can be side effects. If glucose levels stay too high, the body becomes hyperglycemic. Symptoms include blurry vision, tiredness, and frequent urination. If glucose levels sink too low, the body becomes hypoglycemic. Symptoms include dizziness, irritability, and confusion. If either problem goes on too long, a person may have eye, kidney, nerve, and heart problems.

either store glucose as fat or use it for energy right away. Then, glucose levels in the blood drop back to the usual level.

The body also has a system to keep blood sugar levels from dropping too low. The pancreas makes a hormone called glucagon. This hormone tells the liver to change fat into glucose. Then, the glucose is released back into the bloodstream for use. This process makes sure the body has enough blood sugar to keep all of its parts running.

"GOOD" AND "BAD" CARBS

In one sense, the more carbs a person eats, the more energy he or she will have. But that's not the whole story. Carbs are digested at different rates.

The body breaks down simple carbs quickly. Glucose and energy levels rise quickly. Then they suddenly drop. With the fall in blood sugar, hunger and tiredness can return. Many foods with simple carbs also have added sugar. This sugar does not occur naturally in foods. It is added to the food during processing.

DIABETES

Many people's bodies naturally regulate blood sugar. But some people have diabetes. This disease causes trouble with insulin. There are two types of diabetes. People with type 1 diabetes aren't able to make enough insulin. Their immune systems destroy insulin-producing cells. People who suffer from type 2 diabetes resist the effects of insulin. Their bodies need to make more insulin to keep blood glucose levels normal. In both cases, people with diabetes may take daily shots of insulin to stay healthy.

Bean soup can be one good source of complex carbs.

More-nutritious snacks include beans and whole grains. They have complex carbs. Unlike candy or soda, they are also packed with fiber, vitamins, and minerals. These nutrients help keep the body's energy levels steady. The complex carbs in Lucy's breakfast helped her win the race.

Whether simple or complex, carbs are an essential part of a healthy diet. Knowing the facts about carbs and how they affect the body is important. This is the first step to feeling energized and strong. A balanced body is a healthy one.

EXPLORE ONLINE

Chapter One talks about how the body uses carbs. The video at the website below explains what carbs do and how they affect your health. As you know, every source is different. What information does the video give about carbs? How is the information from the video the same as the information in Chapter One? What new information did you learn?

HOW DO CARBOHYDRATES IMPACT YOUR HEALTH?
abdocorelibrary.com/carbohydrates

SIMPLE CARBS

Carbs are found in many foods. They are made of carbon, hydrogen, and oxygen. That's where they get their name. *Carbo* means "carbon" and *hydrate* means "water." Water is made of hydrogen and oxygen.

All carbs exist as molecules or chains of molecules. Simple carbs have the most basic structure. They consist of single sugar molecules called monosaccharides or pairs of sugar molecules called disaccharides. Complex carbs have three or more sugar molecules.

One common myth is that complex carbs are good for you while simple carbs should

Fruits are a common source of simple carbs.

IS FRUIT JUICE HEALTHY?

Whole fruits have nutrients that protect the body against diseases. Juice made from fruit isn't unhealthy. But it's not as good for you as whole fruit. Fruit juice is mostly fructose (sugar) and water. It lacks the fiber found in whole fruit. Fiber slows down digestion and keeps energy levels steady. One orange has 12 grams of sugar and 62 calories. But an eight-ounce (240-mL) cup of fresh orange juice has 21 grams of sugar and 112 calories. Eating whole fruit instead of drinking juice is always a smarter option.

be avoided. But that's not totally true. Some simple carbs can be nutritious. It depends on where they come from and how much you eat.

NATURAL VERSUS ADDED SUGAR

The healthiest types of simple carbs occur naturally in food. For example, fructose is a sugar found in whole fruits. Strawberries, kiwis, and melons have fructose. Lactose is a sugar in milk and yogurt. Each provides the body with the energy it needs.

Treats such as cookies look and taste delicious but are best enjoyed in small portions.

In contrast, some simple carbs are added to food during processing or preparation. They come in many forms. They include white sugar, brown sugar, cane sugar, honey, and maple syrup. These simple carbs are found in treats including cookies, cakes, candy, and some fruit juices.

Many people think sweeteners make food taste delicious. In some cases, sugar makes food last longer on store shelves. But refined sugars have little to no nutritional value. If eaten in large amounts, they can cause problems. They may cause tooth decay, weight gain, and other issues.

HIGH-FRUCTOSE CORN SYRUP

High-fructose corn syrup is one of the main ingredients in many sweetened beverages and breakfast cereals. It's made by processing cornstarch into a sugary glucose syrup. Manufacturers then turn some of the glucose into fructose. Fructose tastes sweeter. High-fructose corn syrup can cause more weight gain than natural sweeteners. The sugar has also been linked to cases of type 2 diabetes.

A common source of added sugar in one's diet is sugary drinks such as sodas.

BOOSTING CARB LEVELS

The US Food and Drug Administration recommends people eat no more than 50 grams of added sugar per day. That's a little more than 12 teaspoons. The average person in the United States eats much more sugar than is recommended. The average American

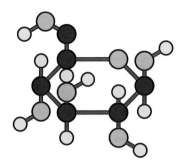

Glucose Molecule

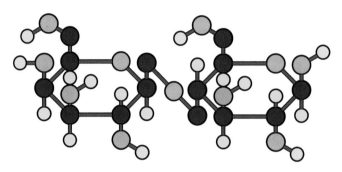

Lactose Molecule Chain

Simple sugar molecules such as glucose can combine with other molecules to create more complex sugars, such as lactose.

consumes 22 teaspoons (88 g) of added sugar a day. That's approximately 66 pounds (30 kg) of added sugar per person each year!

Despite the health risks, consuming food or drinks high in simple carbs can be helpful. But these simple carbs should come from foods such as fruits and vegetables. These foods have other nutrients that help slow down how quickly the body absorbs simple carbs. People should always steer clear of too much added sugar. Food and beverages with complex carbs are the wiser choice.

FURTHER EVIDENCE

Chapter Two talks about simple carbs. Identify one of the chapter's main points. What evidence does the author provide to support this point? The website at the link below discusses one type of simple carb: sugar. Find a quote on this website that supports the main point you identified. Does the quote support an existing piece of evidence in the chapter? Or does it offer a new piece of evidence?

SUGAR: YES, YOU'RE SWEET ENOUGH!
abdocorelibrary.com/carbohydrates

COMPLEX CARBS

Imagine the menu of your favorite restaurant. One dish is spaghetti in a rich tomato sauce. Another is a sizzling pepperoni pizza with whole-wheat crust. A stir-fry with tofu, vegetables, and rice is available too. Each of these dishes is packed full of complex carbs that pump the body full of energy.

Similar to simple carbs, complex carbs need to be broken down before they can be used for energy. Complex carbs have chains of three or more molecules. So it takes longer for the body to break them down than simple carbs. Glucose is gradually released into

Pasta can be a good source of complex carbs.

Sandwiches made with whole-grain bread can help people feel full longer than sandwiches with white bread.

the bloodstream during digestion. This keeps energy levels steady.

As a result, the body feels full for a longer period of time. People who eat meals full of complex carbs are less likely to overeat. They're also not as tempted to snack between meals.

SUPER STARCHES

Complex carbs fall into two main categories. Most are starches. These are found in bread, cereal, pasta, and rice. Some starches are healthier than others. Refined grains, such as white flour and white rice, have been processed. They lack the important nutrients that give the body energy.

Unrefined grains, such as brown rice or whole-wheat flour, are healthier. They are packed with vitamins and minerals. They have iron and B vitamins. Starches are also in some vegetables, including corn, potatoes, parsnips, and green peas.

FABULOUS FIBER

The other type of complex carb is called fiber. It is the part of plant-based food that the small intestine can't digest. There are two kinds of fiber: soluble and insoluble. Both are healthy. During digestion, soluble fiber dissolves in water and forms a gooey substance in the stomach, similar to a gel. This gel travels to the

WHOLE GRAINS

Grains are seeds. There are many different types. A few include barley, corn, millet, oats, rice, and wheat. Whole grains are the healthiest to eat. That's because they include the entire seed. No part is removed during processing. In addition to having lots of dietary fiber, whole grains are also high in vitamins and minerals that help keep the body working well.

large intestine and is partially broken down by bacteria. It helps make you feel full longer. Peas, oatmeal, and apples all have soluble fiber.

Insoluble fiber doesn't dissolve in water. It instead holds water and bulks up. It remains in mostly one piece throughout digestion. Insoluble fiber is found in brown rice, whole grains, vegetables, and many beans.

BOUNTIFUL BENEFITS

Nutritionists recommend most people eat 25 grams of fiber per day. A variety of nutrient-rich foods have fiber. They include unsalted nuts and seeds, colorful

A bowl of oatmeal can provide some of the fiber the body needs.

vegetables, and whole fruits. At least half of the grains someone eats should be whole grains.

Eating fiber has many benefits. Fiber cannot be digested. The digestive system pushes it out of the body as waste. The digestive system can push it out because it is bulky. There are other things the body needs to push out as waste too. But they do not become bulky. So they can only be shed if they

Refined grains are not as healthy to eat as whole grains. Processing removes the nutrient-rich parts. Food manufacturers do this to give the grains a lighter color and finer texture. Removing certain parts also gives grains a longer shelf life. But refined grains have less dietary fiber, iron, vitamin E, and B vitamins than whole grains. They are less nutritious for the body. Refined grains include white rice, white bread, and white flour.

are pushed out with fiber. These include low-density lipoprotein, a form of cholesterol. Large amounts are linked to heart disease. Eating fiber helps the body shed this cholesterol. Fiber also takes a long time to pass through the digestive system. As a result, the body feels fuller longer. Insoluble fiber keeps the digestive system working properly by helping it push food through the intestines. This prevents constipation. Starchy, fibrous foods can have more calories than some other foods. But a diet high in complex carbs protects against heart disease and some forms of cancer.

STRAIGHT TO THE
SOURCE

In a 2004 interview, cardiologist Arthur Agatston discussed which types of carbs are the healthiest to eat:

Basically, whole fruits are very good for you. They have fiber. They have wonderful natural vitamins and nutrients, but when you take a lot of whole fruits and concentrate the juice, that's a problem. . . . That's concentrated sugar. . . .

When you take the fiber out of the bread, again, you're taking the nutrients, the vitamins, and you're left with empty calories that cause large swings in blood sugar. . . . But if you make whole grain bread, which takes longer to chew and to eat and digest, that is fine.

Source: "Interview: Arthur Agatston, M.D." *Frontline: Diet Wars*. WGBH Educational Foundation, January 7, 2004. Web. Accessed September 25, 2018.

Back It Up

The author of this passage is using evidence to support a point. Write a paragraph describing the point the author is making. Then write down two or three pieces of evidence the author uses to make the point.

CHAPTER
FOUR

CARBS AND DIETING

Carbs are the body's major energy suppliers. But they are also one of its main sources of calories. In the United States, 35 percent of men are obese. So are 40 percent of women. Seventeen percent of young people are too. Low-carb diets have become a popular way for people to lose weight. However, this may not be the best approach for most people.

Some of the most well-known low-carb diets are based on the glycemic index (GI). This chart measures how carbs in food affect blood sugar levels. It ranks foods on a scale from 1 to 100. The higher the number, the faster the

Some people eat more vegetables and fewer grains as part of their low-carb diets.

food is digested. This means a greater swing in glucose levels after eating. The feeling of hunger will return more quickly as well.

High-GI foods measure between 70 and 100 on the GI scale. Eating these foods can cause glucose and energy levels to spike then quickly drop. High-GI foods include doughnuts, corn flakes, and french fries.

Medium-GI foods fall in the 56 to 69 range. Some examples are honey, brown rice, and potato chips. Low-GI foods have a rating of 55 or less. They include whole oats, peanuts, and lentils. These foods are digested slowly and steadily. Keeping track of GI

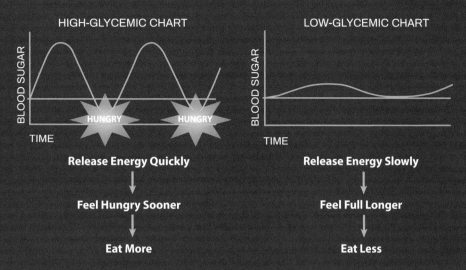

YOUR HEALTH AND THE GI

HIGH-GLYCEMIC CHART

BLOOD SUGAR

TIME

HUNGRY   HUNGRY

LOW-GLYCEMIC CHART

BLOOD SUGAR

TIME

Release Energy Quickly

↓

Feel Hungry Sooner

↓

Eat More

Release Energy Slowly

↓

Feel Full Longer

↓

Eat Less

High-GI carbs cause rapid swings in blood sugar levels. This results in sudden tiredness and hunger. Low-GI carbs help curb weight gain. They control the appetite by delaying hunger. Which blood sugar pattern do you think is healthier, and why?

numbers and eating low-GI foods has helped some people shed pounds.

GI-BASED DIETS

Many GI-based diets suggest substituting carbs with other nutrients in order to lose weight. The South Beach diet calls for getting rid of most refined carbs. People eat protein, healthy fats, and vegetables instead. They eat lower-GI foods. They may eat seafood and tofu.

People who follow the Atkins diet eat a lot of red meat, eggs, or chicken at every meal. Most breads, fruits, grains, and nuts are off-limits. That's because people on this diet rely on fat and protein instead of carbs for energy. Both South Beach and Atkins dieters reintroduce some whole grains and fruits in later stages.

But severely restricting carbs can cause problems for some people. Normally, the body burns carbs for energy. Without carbs, the body goes into a state called ketosis. There are not enough carbs for the body to use. So the body uses fat for energy. Long-term ketosis can cause mental fogginess, dehydration, and severe headaches.

THE BOTTOM LINE

In 2015, the US government recommended that carbs make up 45 to 65 percent of a person's total daily calorie intake. The guidelines calculate amounts of nutrients, called daily values, using 2,000 calories a day. A person following the guidelines would aim for between 900 and 1,300 calories a day from carbs.

But many people eat less. The main idea behind any low-carb diet is that cutting back on carbs decreases a person's calorie intake and lowers insulin levels. This causes the body to burn stored fat for energy instead of glucose. Carbs help the body hold on to water. During the first few days of a low-carb diet, the body loses water. So the initial weight loss is mostly water weight. Long-term dieting can be difficult to sustain.

PROBLEMS WITH THE GI

Many people adopt GI-based diets to lose weight or to control blood sugar levels. But some doctors say this method isn't always reliable. A food's GI value doesn't take into account how it is prepared or processed. It also doesn't consider information about other nutrients in the food. For example, whole milk has a value of 31 for an eight-ounce (240-mL) serving. It is low on the GI scale. But whole milk also has a lot of fat. Too much fat is unhealthy. Just because a food has a low GI value doesn't mean it is a good option for losing weight.

Amount per 1 cup

Calories 250

% DV*

11%	**Total Fat** 7g
16%	**Saturated Fat** 3g
	Trans **Fat** 0g
2%	**Cholesterol** 4mg
13%	**Sodium** 300mg
10%	**Total Carbs** 30g
14%	**Dietary Fiber** 3g
	Sugars 2g
	Added Sugars 0g
	Protein 5g

Nutrition labels show how many carbs are in a product. They also show the amount of sugar and fiber.

Finding the right diet can be difficult. Some people cut out carbs for a short period in order to stay trim or better their health. Others work at it for years without showing results. In the end, dieting is best handled using a balanced approach. Cutting out one type of nutrient isn't always healthy. Instead, exercising and reducing calories by choosing healthier foods is key.

STRAIGHT TO THE
SOURCE

Dr. David Ludwig is a professor in the Department of Nutrition at Harvard's School of Public Health. He discussed GI diets in a 2015 interview:

The bottom line is that GI has been extremely useful in the research setting for characterizing carbohydrate quality. But for most people, there's no need to "eat by the numbers"— either glycemic index, total calories or any other scale. Choosing whole instead of highly processed carbohydrates will naturally result in a low GI diet that will also have many other nutritious aspects including high content of fiber, vitamins, [and] minerals. . . . (Note: Use of GI as a guide to food selection may have specific benefit for people with diabetes or other severe metabolic problems.)

Source: "Dr. David Ludwig Clears Up Carbohydrate Confusion." *Harvard T. H. Chan School of Public Health*. President and Fellows of Harvard College, December 16, 2015. Web. Accessed September 26, 2018.

What's the Big Idea?
Read this quote carefully. What is its main idea? Name two or three details that are used to support the main idea.

A HEALTHY BALANCE

There are lots of ways to include carbs in your daily diet. As with most things in life, moderation is important. The more balanced your approach, the healthier you'll be.

Start by thinking about what you eat and drink every day. Cut back on foods and beverages high in simple carbs. Instead, choose foods that have complex carbs whenever possible. Remember to prioritize whole foods over empty calories too. That means saying no to a slice of bologna on white bread with a can of soda.

One way to eat healthy is to replace sugary foods with naturally sweet foods like strawberries.

THE HEALTHY EATING PLATE

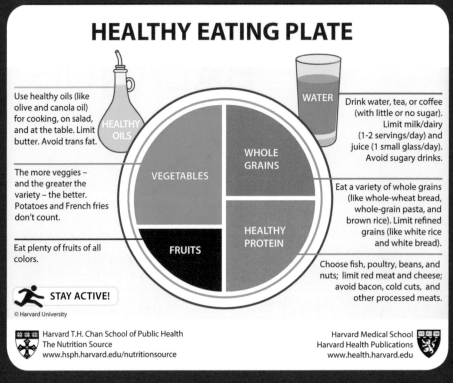

HEALTHY EATING PLATE

Use healthy oils (like olive and canola oil) for cooking, on salad, and at the table. Limit butter. Avoid trans fat.

HEALTHY OILS

WATER

Drink water, tea, or coffee (with little or no sugar). Limit milk/dairy (1-2 servings/day) and juice (1 small glass/day). Avoid sugary drinks.

The more veggies – and the greater the variety – the better. Potatoes and French fries don't count.

VEGETABLES

WHOLE GRAINS

Eat a variety of whole grains (like whole-wheat bread, whole-grain pasta, and brown rice). Limit refined grains (like white rice and white bread).

Eat plenty of fruits of all colors.

FRUITS

HEALTHY PROTEIN

Choose fish, poultry, beans, and nuts; limit red meat and cheese; avoid bacon, cold cuts, and other processed meats.

🏃 **STAY ACTIVE!**

© Harvard University

Harvard T.H. Chan School of Public Health
The Nutrition Source
www.hsph.harvard.edu/nutritionsource

Harvard Medical School
Harvard Health Publications
www.health.harvard.edu

Nutrition experts at Harvard's T. H. Chan School of Public Health created the Healthy Eating Plate. It provides guidance on how to make the best possible eating choices. What would you pack for your school lunch based on this guide?

Instead, eat whole-grain crackers with peanut butter and a glass of water or unsweetened tea.

Next, try avoiding overly processed foods, such as potato chips or sweetened breakfast cereals. Packaged food is usually high in fat, salt, and added sugars.

Many processed foods also have few nutrients compared to the number of calories they provide. The more you focus on what you put in your body every time you eat, the easier it'll become to maintain a healthy diet.

HOW YOU EAT

It's important to think about how you eat too. Stuffing your stomach with fries and potato chips all day long might taste great. But filling up on too many carbs, even the healthy complex kind, can lead to weight gain. That's because the body is getting more calories than it actually needs.

DON'T SKIP BREAKFAST!

Many people skip breakfast in the morning. That isn't a healthy habit. People who eat breakfast tend to have lower rates of heart disease, high blood pressure, and high cholesterol. But that doesn't mean eating a sugary pastry every day is a good idea. Instead, whole-grain toast with peanut butter is a great energy booster to begin your morning. A bowl of oatmeal or shredded wheat has plenty of fiber and is low in calories.

LOOK AT NUTRITION LABELS

Nutrition labels explain what's in the food you eat. Percentages of carbs, fats, and other nutrients are listed on most packaged foods and even on menus in some restaurants. These percentages are based on a 2,000-calorie adult diet. Ingredients are also listed on nutrition labels. Make sure to pay attention to serving size and the amount of servings per container or package. That way you'll be able to keep your portions in check. If you need help reading the label, ask an adult for help.

Eating regular, balanced meals is critical. Sitting down for a balanced breakfast, lunch, and dinner helps you feel full and energized throughout the day. You'll also be less tempted to gobble down fattening snacks since you won't feel as hungry.

Two other things to keep in mind are nutrition labels and portion control. Find out what is in your food by reading nutrition labels. Then, eat what you take. This cuts back on waste. Get a sense of how much food your body really needs and take only what you will eat. There can be health risks in the long run if overeating becomes a habit.

DON'T FORGET TO EXERCISE

One of the most important things to remember is that staying healthy involves the whole body, not just your diet. Being active goes hand in hand with eating the right foods. Find an activity you like. Play soccer. Try a gymnastics class. Plan a softball game with some friends. Regular exercise is necessary to use carbs properly.

Thinking positively and being open to new experiences helps too. Research some of the health benefits of certain foods. Also look up the risks of eating some foods. Try to eat more healthy foods and be more active every day.

Above everything else, pay attention to your nutrition. Consistently getting the right vitamins, minerals, and carbs is important to feeling your best. After all, you are what you eat.

FAST FACTS

- Carbohydrates, or carbs, are substances found in certain types of food that provide the body with energy.

- Carbs are made up of carbon, hydrogen, and oxygen.

- There are two main types of carbs: simple and complex.

- Simple carbs are mostly sugars.

- Complex carbs are either starches or fiber.

- The body uses carbs by breaking them down into a sugar called glucose.

- The glycemic index is a system that rates foods on a scale from 1 to 100 based on their effect on blood sugar levels. Foods with higher numbers digest quickly and cause spikes in blood sugar. Foods with lower numbers digest slowly and help people feel full longer.

- Eating too many simple carbs can cause weight gain, and the extra calories in these foods are linked to certain chronic diseases.

STOP AND
THINK

Say What?

Studying carbohydrates and how they affect the body can mean learning a lot of new vocabulary. Find five words in this book you've never heard before. Use a dictionary to find out what they mean. Then write the meanings in your own words, and use each word in a new sentence.

Why Do I Care?

Maybe you are happy with the foods you eat. But that doesn't mean you can't think about healthier ways to eat. How does eating carbohydrates affect the way your body feels? Do you have friends or family members who are cutting back on carbs for health reasons? How might your life be different if you replaced one food high in carbohydrates per day with something else?

Another View

Chapter Five gives recommendations about how to maintain a healthy diet. As you know, every source is different. Ask an adult to help you find another source that discusses how

to stay healthy and fit. Write a short essay comparing and contrasting the new source's point of view with that of this book's author. What is the point of view of each author? How are they similar and why? How are they different and why?

Surprise Me

Chapter One explains how the body processes carbohydrates and converts them into glucose to use as energy. After reading this book, what two or three facts about this process did you find most surprising? Write a few sentences about each fact. Why did you find each fact surprising?

GLOSSARY

calorie
a unit that measures the amount of energy a food produces when it's taken into the body

digestion
the process of breaking down food into substances that can be used by the body

hormone
a substance made by cells in the body that helps control body processes, such as growth

metabolic
having to do with metabolism, the processes in plants and animals that take place when food is changed into energy or used to make cells and tissues

moderation
the act of avoiding extreme highs and lows

molecule
the smallest unit of a chemical compound

nutrient
something in food that helps people, animals, and plants live and grow

obese
the state of being very overweight

processed
having gone through manufacturing

refined
having been altered through processing and made less nutritious

ONLINE
RESOURCES

To learn more about your body on carbohydrates, visit our free resource websites below.

Visit **abdocorelibrary.com** or scan this QR code for free Common Core resources for teachers and students, including vetted activities, multimedia, and booklinks, for deeper subject comprehension.

Visit **abdobooklinks.com** or scan this QR code for free additional online weblinks for further learning. These links are routinely monitored and updated to provide the most current information available.

LEARN
MORE

Are You What You Eat? New York: DK, 2015. Print.

Reinke, Beth Bence. *Nutrition Basics.* Minneapolis, MN: Abdo Publishing, 2016. Print.

INDEX

About the Author

Alexis Burling has written more than 25 nonfiction books for young readers. She is also a book critic with reviews published in the *New York Times*, *San Francisco Chronicle*, and other publications. She lives with her husband in the Pacific Northwest.